NICKOS IV

JOURNEY OF THE LENS

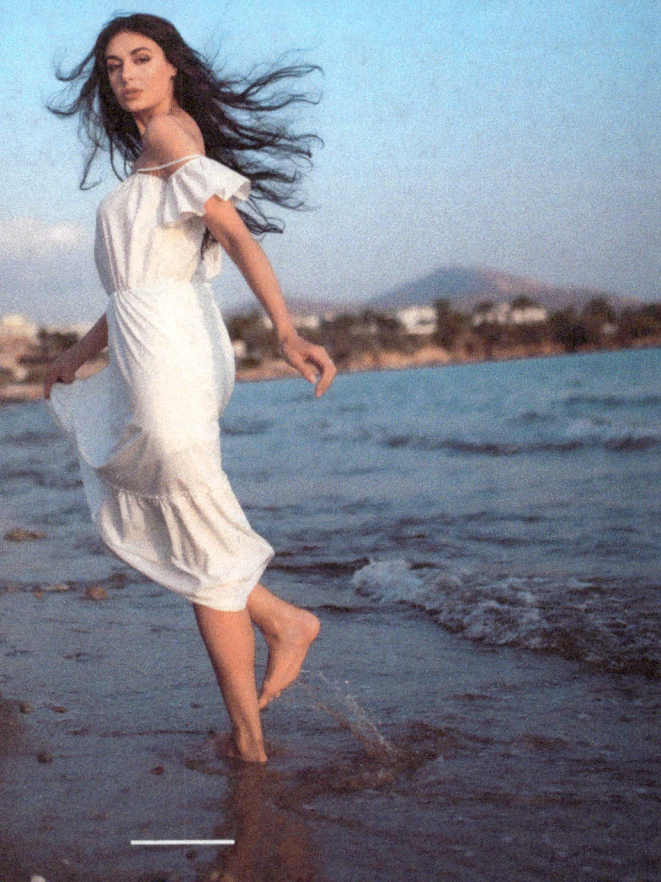

Capturing Life Through the Lens:
A Comprehensive Guide to Photography

Introduction

Welcome to "Journey of the Lens: A Comprehensive Guide to Photography." Photography is a captivating art form that allows us to capture the beauty and essence of the world around us. Whether you're an amateur photographer just starting out or a seasoned professional looking to enhance your skills, this book is for you.

In the following chapters, we'll explore the different types of photography, understanding your camera and its features, composition and framing techniques, and lighting tips and tricks. You'll learn how to take stunning photos that capture your vision and tell your story.

This book is designed to be a comprehensive guide to photography, covering everything from the basics to more advanced techniques. With practical tips and real-world examples, you'll gain the knowledge and confidence you need to take your photography to the next level.

So, grab your camera, and let's embark on this journey of the lens together!

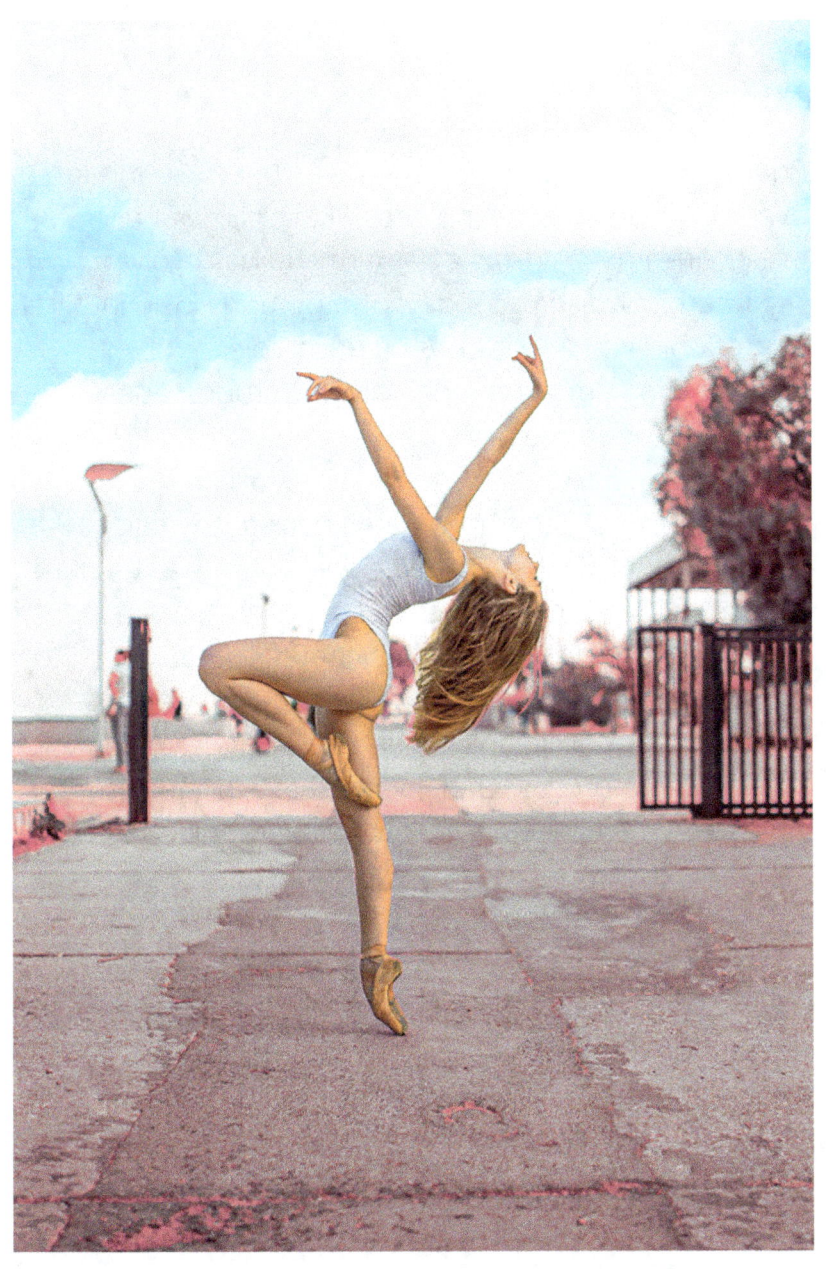

Chapter 1: Introduction to Photography

Photography is a form of art that has been around for over 180 years. It is the process of capturing and preserving images using a camera and has evolved significantly over time. Today, photography is an integral part of our lives, and it plays a critical role in documenting our experiences, telling stories, and preserving memories.

The history of photography dates back to the early 19th century when the first photographic image was created by Joseph Nicéphore Niépce in 1826. The process involved exposing a metal plate coated with bitumen to light, creating a unique image that could be viewed under certain conditions. Later, Louis Daguerre improved the process and invented the daguerreotype, which was the first widely used photographic process.

Over the years, photography has evolved significantly, with the invention of new technologies and advancements in camera technology. Today, we have a wide range of cameras available, from high-end DSLRs to smartphones with impressive cameras.

There are many types of photography, each requiring a different set of skills and equipment. Some of the most popular genres of photography include:

Landscape Photography: This type of photography involves capturing the natural beauty of the world around us, such as mountains, oceans, forests, and more.

Portrait Photography: Portrait photography involves capturing images of people, either in a studio or in natural surroundings.

Wildlife Photography: This type of photography involves capturing images of animals in their natural habitats.

Macro Photography: Macro photography involves capturing images of small objects or subjects, such as insects or flowers, in extreme detail.

Street Photography: Street photography involves capturing images of people and places in public spaces, such as streets, parks, and cities.

The importance of photography in our lives cannot be overstated. It allows us to capture and preserve memories, document historic events, and tell stories. Photography is an essential tool for businesses, allowing them to market and promote their products and services effectively. Additionally, photography can have a significant impact on our emotions and how we perceive the world around us.

Photography has also become an essential tool for social media and communication. With the rise of social media platforms like Instagram, Facebook, and Snapchat, photography has become an essential means of communication and self-expression. We use photographs to share our experiences with others, tell stories, and express ourselves creatively.

In conclusion, photography is an art form that has evolved significantly over the years. It has become an integral part of our lives, allowing us to capture and preserve our memories, document important events, and tell stories. With the advent of new technologies, photography will continue to evolve, and we can look forward to capturing even more incredible moments in the years to come.

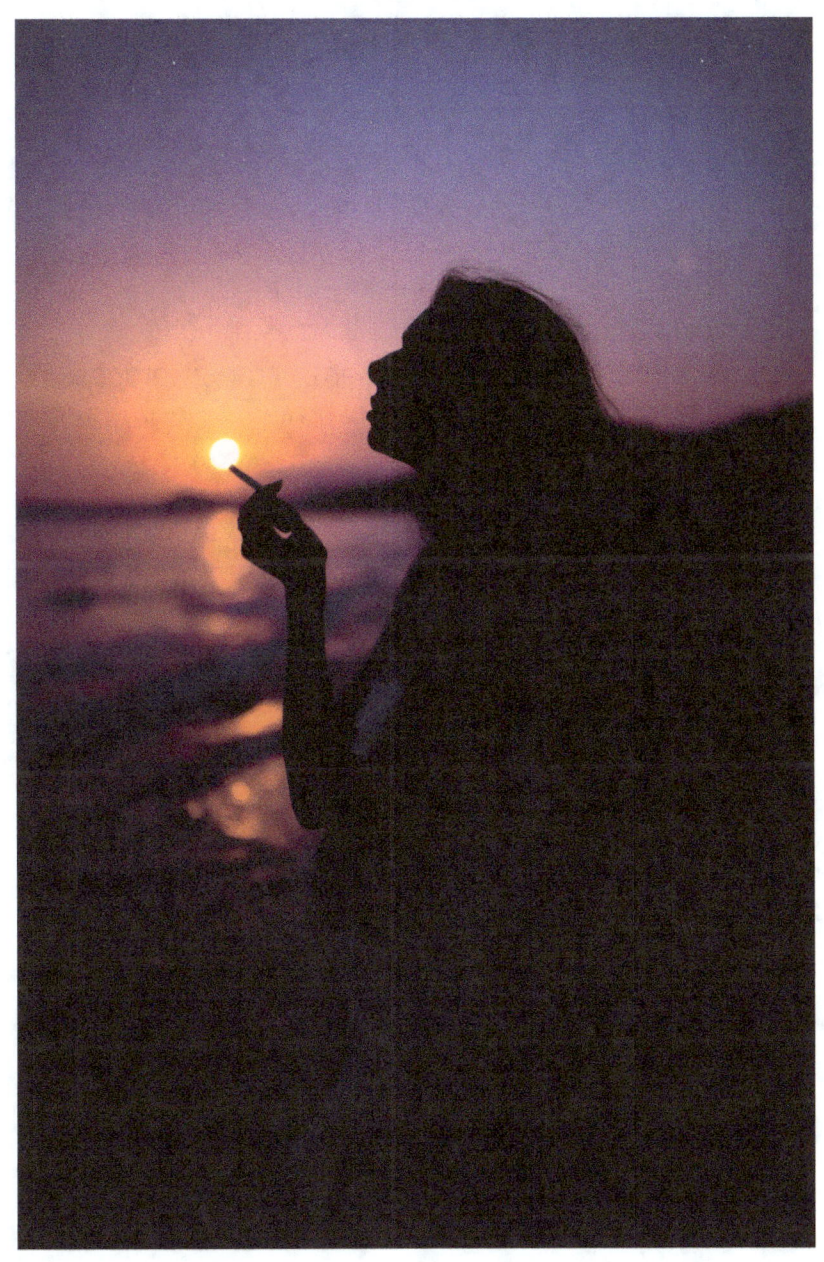

Chapter 2: Understanding Your Camera

Photography is a beautiful art that allows us to capture and preserve memories, moments, and beauty. Whether you are a professional or an amateur, it is essential to understand your camera to produce the best images possible. In this chapter, we will discuss the different types of cameras, parts of a camera, camera settings and modes, and tips for choosing the right camera.

Types of Cameras

There are various types of cameras available in the market, each with its own unique features and specifications. Here are some of the most popular camera types:

Point-and-Shoot Cameras: These are the simplest cameras, also known as compact cameras. They are designed to be easy to use and carry around. Point-and-shoot cameras are perfect for beginners or those who want a camera for everyday use.

DSLR Cameras: DSLR stands for Digital Single-Lens Reflex. These cameras use a mirror and prism system to capture images. They offer more control over settings, interchangeable lenses, and high-quality images.

Mirrorless Cameras: These cameras are similar to DSLRs, but they do not have a mirror and prism system. Instead, they use an electronic viewfinder to preview the image. Mirrorless cameras are lighter and more compact than DSLRs and offer high-quality images.

Medium Format Cameras: These cameras use larger sensors, resulting in better image quality and detail. They are popular among professional photographers and are commonly used in fashion, portrait, and landscape photography.

Film Cameras: Film cameras use film to capture images instead of digital sensors. They are popular among film enthusiasts and are often used for artistic and creative purposes.

Parts of a Camera

Before delving into camera settings and modes, it is essential to understand the different parts of a camera. Here are the essential components of a camera:

Lens: The lens is the most critical part of a camera. It controls the amount of light that enters the camera and focuses the light onto the sensor.

Sensor: The sensor is the part of the camera that captures the image. It is the digital equivalent of film in film cameras.

Shutter: The shutter controls the amount of time the sensor is exposed to light. It opens and closes quickly, allowing the sensor to capture the image.

Aperture: The aperture controls the amount of light that enters the camera. It is measured in f-stops and is represented by a series of numbers. A smaller f-stop number means a larger aperture and more light entering the camera.

ISO: ISO determines the camera's sensitivity to light. A higher ISO means the camera is more sensitive to light and is ideal for low-light situations.

Viewfinder: The viewfinder is where you look through to compose your shot. It can be an optical viewfinder or an electronic viewfinder, depending on the camera type.

Camera Settings and Modes

Now that we have discussed the different camera types and parts let's delve into camera settings and modes.

Shooting Modes: Most cameras come with different shooting modes that are designed to suit various situations. The most common shooting modes are Auto, Manual, Aperture Priority, Shutter Priority, and Program Mode.

Aperture: The aperture controls the depth of field in an image. A large aperture (small f-stop number) will produce a shallow depth of field, while a small aperture (large f-stop number) will produce a deeper depth of field.

Shutter Speed: The shutter speed controls the length of time the sensor is exposed to light. A fast shutter speed will freeze the action, while a slow shutter speed will create motion blur.

ISO: The ISO controls the camera's sensitivity to light. A higher ISO is ideal for low-light situations, while a lower ISO is ideal for bright situations

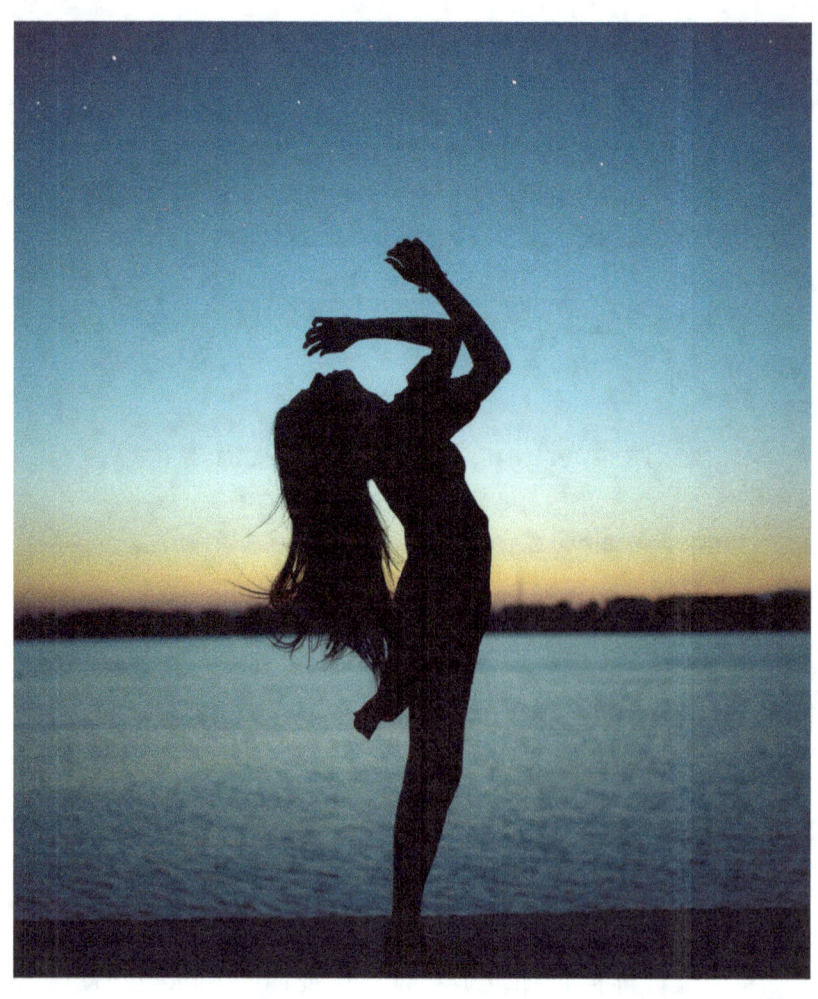

Chapter 3: Composition and Framing

Composition and framing are crucial elements of photography that can make or break a picture. They are the foundation of creating visually appealing and engaging images. In this chapter, we will discuss some essential composition and framing techniques, including the rule of thirds, leading lines, symmetry and balance, and framing techniques.

Rule of Thirds

The rule of thirds is one of the most well-known and commonly used composition techniques. It involves dividing the image into thirds both horizontally and vertically, creating nine equal parts. The idea is to place the subject or point of interest at the intersection of these lines.

The rule of thirds helps create balance and visual interest in the image by preventing the subject from being placed in the center. It also allows the viewer's eyes to move around the image, exploring the scene.

Leading Lines

Leading lines are another popular composition technique that involves using lines in the image to draw the viewer's eyes towards the subject. These lines can be straight or curved, horizontal or vertical, and can be created by natural or man-made elements in the scene.

Leading lines can be used to create a sense of depth, movement, and direction in the image. They can be found in roads, paths, fences, bridges, or even the horizon.

Symmetry and Balance

Symmetry and balance are composition techniques that involve creating a sense of harmony and order in the image. Symmetry is when an image is mirrored or reflected, creating a sense of balance and harmony. It is commonly found in architectural and natural scenes.

Balance is about arranging the elements in the image in a way that creates a sense of equilibrium. It can be achieved by balancing the subject with negative space or using similar elements on both sides of the image.

Framing Techniques

Framing is a technique that involves using elements in the scene to frame the subject. It can be natural, such as trees, arches, or windows, or man-made, such as doorways or fences.

Framing techniques can create a sense of depth, perspective, and focus on the subject. It also adds context and visual interest to the image.

Other composition techniques include the use of color, texture, and patterns to create visual interest in the image. It is essential to experiment with these techniques and find what works best for the scene and subject.

Tips for Framing and Composition

Here are some tips for improving your framing and composition skills:

Take your time: Take the time to explore the scene and find the best angle and composition.

Experiment with different techniques: Don't be afraid to experiment with different techniques to find what works best for the subject.

Look for natural frames: Look for natural frames in the scene, such as arches, trees, or windows.

Use negative space: Negative space is the empty space around the subject. Use it to create balance and focus on the subject.

Be aware of the background: Pay attention to the background to ensure it does not distract from the subject.

Use perspective: Use perspective to create depth and visual interest in the image.

Break the rules: While it is essential to understand composition rules, don't be afraid to break them and create something unique and creative.

In conclusion, framing and composition are essential elements of photography that can take an image from good to great. By understanding these techniques and experimenting with them, you can create visually appealing and engaging images that tell a story and evoke emotion in the viewer.

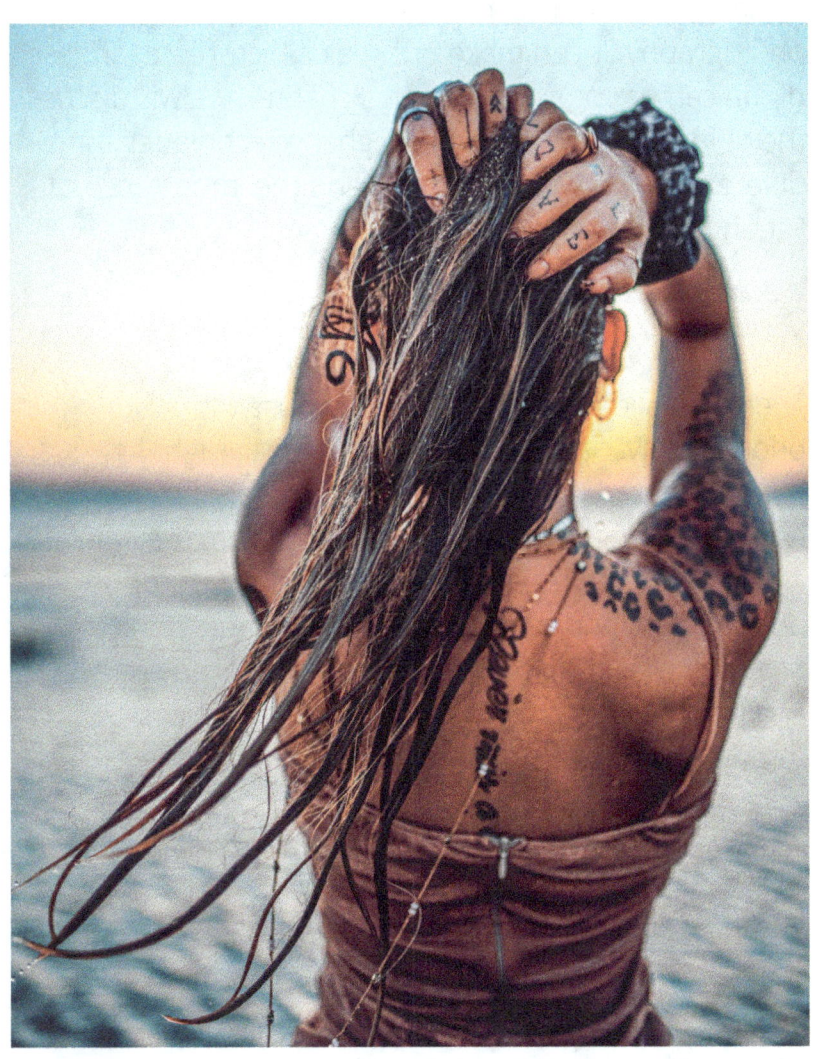

Chapter 4: Lighting

Lighting is one of the most critical elements of photography. It can make or break a picture, regardless of the camera or subject. In this chapter, we will discuss the different types of lighting, lighting techniques for different types of photography, and the importance of lighting in photography.

Types of Lighting

There are two main types of lighting used in photography: natural lighting and artificial lighting.

Natural lighting is the light that comes from the sun, and it is free and readily available. It is ideal for outdoor photography and can create a warm, natural look to the image. However, natural lighting can be unpredictable, and it is essential to understand how it changes throughout the day and how it affects the subject.

Artificial lighting is any type of light that is not natural. It includes studio lights, lamps, flashes, and other types of lighting used to create a specific mood or effect in the image. Artificial lighting is commonly used in portrait and product photography, where the lighting needs to be controlled and consistent.

Lighting Techniques

Different types of photography require different lighting techniques to create the desired effect. Here are some popular lighting techniques for different types of photography:

Portrait Photography: In portrait photography, the focus is on the subject's face and features. It is essential to use soft, diffused lighting to create a flattering, natural look. One popular technique is using a window as the primary light source, creating a soft and even light on the subject's face.

Product Photography: Product photography requires precise lighting to showcase the product's details and features. Using a lightbox or shooting in a well-lit studio with multiple light sources can help control the lighting and create a consistent look across all images.

Landscape Photography: Landscape photography often relies on natural lighting and is typically shot during the golden hour or blue hour. During these times, the light is soft and warm, creating a beautiful and natural look to the image.

Importance of Lighting in Photography

Lighting plays a crucial role in photography, and understanding how it affects the image is essential for creating visually stunning pictures. Here are some reasons why lighting is crucial in photography:

Sets the mood: Lighting can set the mood and tone of the image, creating a specific emotion or feeling.

Highlights the subject: Lighting can highlight the subject's features and details, making it the focal point of the image.

Adds depth: Lighting can add depth and dimension to the image, creating a sense of space and perspective.

Creates contrast: Lighting can create contrast and shadows, adding visual interest and texture to the image.

Evokes emotion: Lighting can evoke emotion in the viewer, creating a powerful and impactful image.

In conclusion, lighting is a crucial element of photography that can make or break a picture. Understanding the different types of lighting and how to control it is essential for creating visually stunning and emotionally impactful images. Experimenting with different lighting techniques and understanding how it affects the subject and mood of the image can help elevate your photography skills.

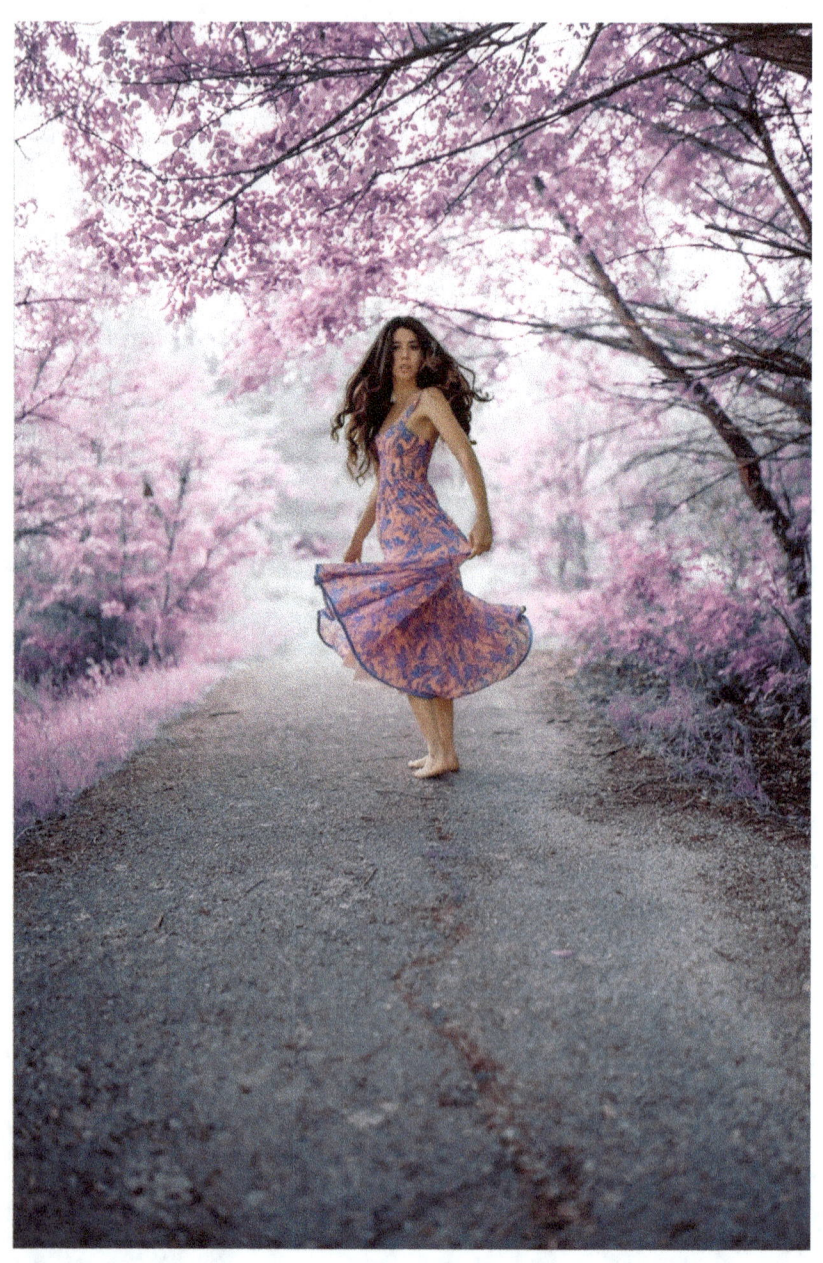

Chapter 5: Exposure and ISO

Exposure is one of the most critical aspects of photography. It refers to the amount of light that enters the camera and affects the brightness and clarity of the image. In this chapter, we will discuss the basics of exposure, including aperture and shutter speed, ISO settings, and tips for achieving proper exposure.

Understanding Exposure

Exposure is the amount of light that enters the camera and affects the brightness and clarity of the image. It is determined by three main factors: aperture, shutter speed, and ISO settings.

Aperture and Shutter Speed

Aperture refers to the opening of the lens through which light enters the camera. It is measured in f-stops, with a smaller f-stop number indicating a larger opening and more light entering the camera. Aperture also affects the depth of field, or the area of the image that is in focus. A larger aperture (smaller f-stop number) creates a shallow depth of field, while a smaller aperture (larger f-stop number) creates a deeper depth of field.

Shutter speed refers to the amount of time that the camera's shutter is open and determines how much light enters the camera. It is measured in seconds or fractions of a second, with a faster shutter speed allowing less light to enter the camera and a slower shutter speed allowing more light to enter the camera. Shutter speed also affects motion blur, with a faster shutter speed freezing motion and a slower shutter speed creating a sense of motion blur.

ISO Settings

ISO refers to the sensitivity of the camera's image sensor to light. A higher ISO setting makes the sensor more sensitive to light, allowing for faster shutter speeds and smaller apertures, but also introducing more noise (graininess) in the image. A lower ISO setting makes the sensor less sensitive to light, resulting in a slower shutter speed and larger aperture but also producing a cleaner, less noisy image.

Tips for Achieving Proper Exposure

Achieving proper exposure is essential for creating high-quality images. Here are some tips for achieving proper exposure:

Understand the exposure triangle: Understanding the relationship between aperture, shutter speed, and ISO settings is critical for achieving proper exposure.

Use the camera's light meter: The camera's light meter measures the light in the scene and helps determine the proper exposure.

Experiment with different settings: Experimenting with different aperture, shutter speed, and ISO settings can help you find the optimal settings for different lighting conditions and subjects.

Use exposure compensation: Exposure compensation allows you to adjust the exposure in the camera's automatic or semi-automatic mode to compensate for different lighting conditions.

Consider shooting in RAW format: Shooting in RAW format allows you to adjust the exposure in post-processing, giving you more flexibility and control over the final image.

In conclusion, understanding exposure is essential for creating high-quality images. Aperture, shutter speed, and ISO settings are the three main factors that affect exposure, and understanding how to control them can help you achieve proper exposure in different lighting conditions and subjects. Experimenting with different settings, using the camera's light meter, and considering shooting in RAW format can help you achieve optimal exposure and create visually stunning images.

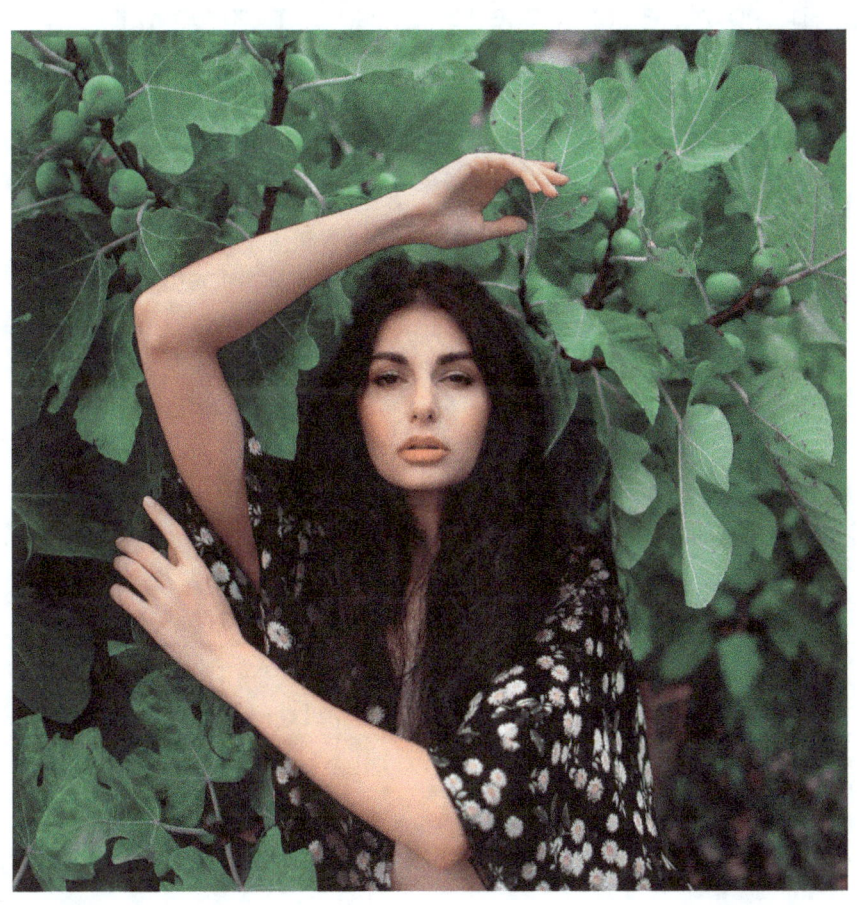

Chapter 6: Color and White Balance

Color is an essential aspect of photography that can greatly impact the mood and overall feel of an image. In this chapter, we will discuss color theory, white balance, and how to adjust white balance in-camera, as well as editing techniques for color correction.

Color Theory

Color theory refers to the principles and guidelines used to create aesthetically pleasing color combinations. It involves understanding the color wheel, which consists of primary colors (red, blue, and yellow), secondary colors (green, orange, and purple), and tertiary colors (created by mixing primary and secondary colors).

Complementary colors, which are opposite each other on the color wheel (such as red and green), create a sense of contrast and can make an image pop. Analogous colors, which are next to each other on the color wheel (such as blue and purple), create a sense of harmony and can be used to create a calming mood.

White Balance and Its Importance

White balance refers to the color temperature of the light in a scene, which can affect the colors in the image. The human eye naturally adjusts to different lighting conditions, but cameras need to be manually adjusted for proper white balance.

Proper white balance is essential for accurate color reproduction in an image. If the white balance is incorrect, the image can have a color cast, where the image appears overly blue or yellow.

How to Adjust White Balance in-Camera

Most cameras have a white balance setting that can be adjusted to match the lighting conditions of the scene. Some common white balance settings include daylight, cloudy, shade, tungsten, and fluorescent.

In addition to these presets, many cameras also have a custom white balance setting, which allows you to manually set the white balance based on a neutral object in the scene, such as a white or gray card.

Editing Techniques for Color Correction

Editing software, such as Adobe Lightroom or Photoshop, can be used to correct color in an image. Here are some editing techniques for color correction:

Adjusting temperature and tint: Temperature adjusts the overall warmth or coolness of the image, while tint adjusts the green or magenta color cast. Adjusting these settings can help balance the colors in the image.

Using the color picker tool: The color picker tool allows you to select a specific color in the image and adjust its hue, saturation, and luminance.

Adjusting individual color channels: Many editing software programs allow you to adjust the red, green, and blue channels individually to fine-tune the color balance in the image.

Using presets: Presets can be used to quickly adjust the color in an image. Many preset packs are available online, and they can be a useful starting point for editing.

In conclusion, color is an essential aspect of photography that can greatly impact the mood and overall feel of an image. Understanding color theory and white balance can help you create visually stunning images with accurate color reproduction. Adjusting white balance in-camera and using editing techniques for color correction can help fine-tune the color balance in an image and make it more visually appealing.

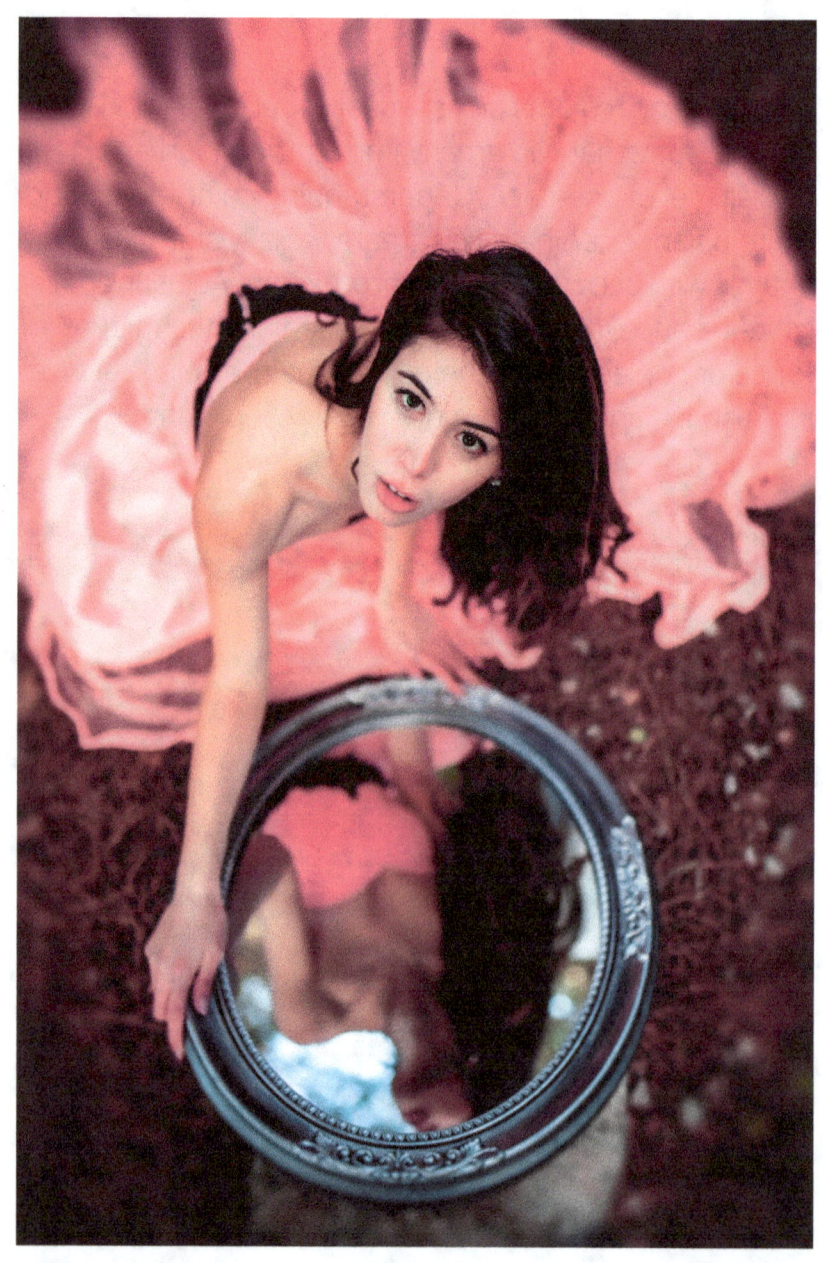

Chapter 7: Focusing Techniques

Achieving sharp focus is critical to producing high-quality images, and in this chapter, we will discuss different focusing techniques to help you capture sharp images. We will cover autofocus and manual focus, focus modes, tips for achieving sharp focus, and techniques for selective focus.

Autofocus and Manual Focus

Most modern cameras are equipped with autofocus systems that use a combination of contrast detection and phase detection to focus on the subject. Autofocus makes it easier to capture sharp images, especially when photographing moving subjects.

On the other hand, manual focus requires the photographer to adjust the focus ring on the lens to achieve sharp focus manually. Manual focus can be challenging, but it gives the photographer greater control over the focus point.

Focus Modes

Most cameras have several focus modes, including single autofocus (AF-S), continuous autofocus (AF-C), and automatic autofocus (AF-A).

Single autofocus mode is used when the subject is stationary, and the photographer wants to capture a single shot. In contrast, continuous autofocus mode is used when the subject is moving, and the photographer needs to capture multiple shots. Automatic autofocus mode switches between single and continuous autofocus modes depending on the scene.

In addition to these basic modes, many cameras also have more advanced autofocus modes, such as face detection autofocus, which detects and focuses on human faces in the scene.

Tips for Achieving Sharp Focus

Use a tripod: A tripod can help stabilize the camera, reducing camera shake and producing sharper images.

Use a fast shutter speed: Using a faster shutter speed can reduce the impact of camera shake and produce sharper images, especially when photographing moving subjects.

Use the right focus mode: Select the appropriate focus mode for the scene, such as single autofocus for stationary subjects and continuous autofocus for moving subjects.

Use the right autofocus point: Selecting the right autofocus point ensures that the camera focuses on the subject accurately.

Use manual focus: Manual focus can be challenging, but it gives you greater control over the focus point, especially in low-light conditions.

Techniques for Selective Focus

Selective focus refers to a technique where a specific part of the image is in focus, while the rest of the image is blurred. Selective focus can be used to draw attention to the subject, create a sense of depth, or add a sense of mystery to the image.

Here are some techniques for achieving selective focus:

Use a wide aperture: Using a wide aperture (such as f/1.8 or f/2.8) creates a shallow depth of field, resulting in a blurred background.

Use a telephoto lens: Telephoto lenses have a narrow field of view, allowing you to isolate the subject and blur the background.

Use manual focus: Manual focus allows you to select the specific point of focus, resulting in a selective focus effect.

Use post-processing: Selective focus can also be achieved in post-processing using techniques such as Gaussian blur or the tilt-shift effect.

In conclusion, achieving sharp focus is critical to producing high-quality images, and understanding different focusing techniques can help you capture sharp images. Autofocus and manual focus have their advantages and disadvantages, and using the right focus mode and focus point can help you achieve sharp focus. Selective focus can be achieved using techniques such as using a wide aperture, telephoto lens, or manual focus. With practice and experimentation, you can master focusing techniques and create visually stunning images.

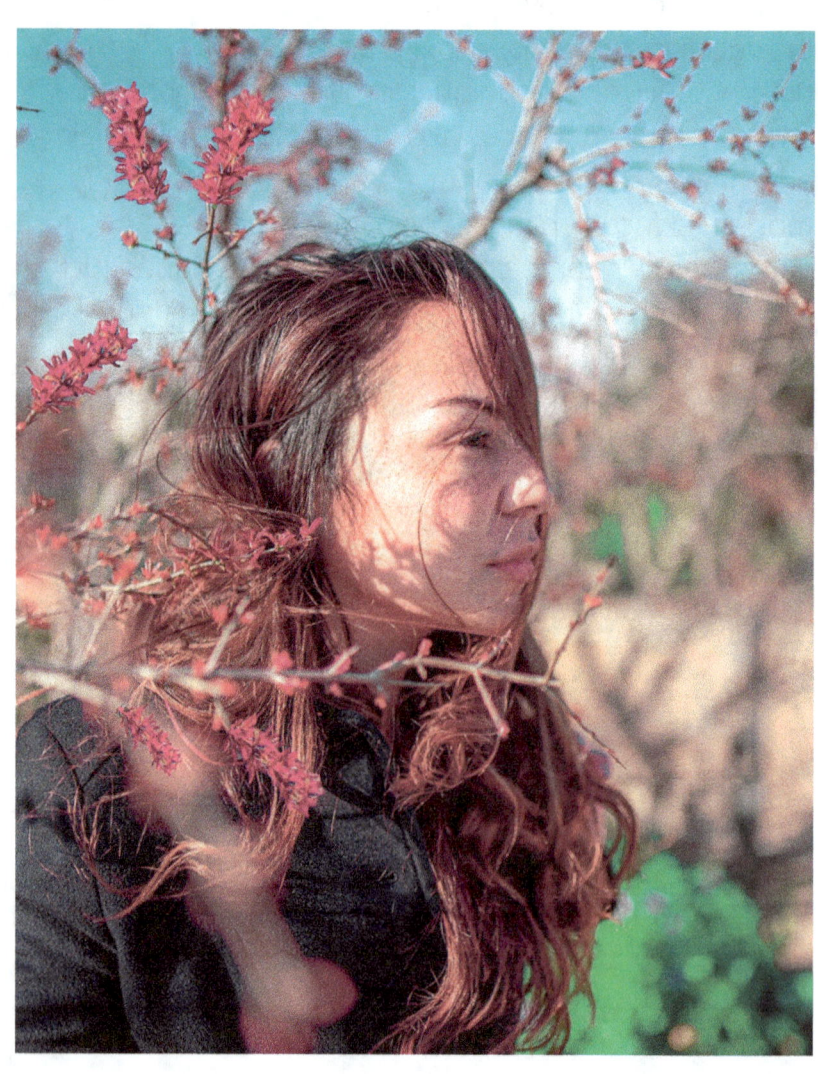

Chapter 8: Post-Processing

Post-processing is an essential part of digital photography, and it involves using editing software to enhance and manipulate the images captured by your camera. In this chapter, we will discuss the types of post-processing software, basic and advanced editing techniques, and tips for achieving a consistent editing style.

Types of Post-Processing Software

There are many post-processing software available on the market, ranging from free options to expensive professional-grade software. Here are some popular post-processing software:

Adobe Photoshop: Adobe Photoshop is one of the most popular photo editing software, widely used by professional photographers and graphic designers. It offers a wide range of tools for image manipulation, from basic editing to advanced retouching.

Lightroom: Adobe Lightroom is a photo management and editing software that is designed for photographers. It offers a range of tools for organizing, editing, and sharing photos.

Capture One: Capture One is a professional-grade photo editing software that offers advanced color grading tools and RAW file processing capabilities.

GIMP: GIMP (GNU Image Manipulation Program) is a free and open-source photo editing software that offers a range of tools for basic editing and retouching.

Basic Editing Techniques

Basic editing techniques involve adjusting the exposure, color, and contrast of the image to enhance its visual appeal. Here are some basic editing techniques:

Adjusting exposure: Exposure refers to the amount of light that enters the camera sensor when taking a photo. Adjusting the exposure can help brighten or darken the image.

Adjusting color balance: Color balance refers to the relative amounts of different colors in the image. Adjusting the color balance can help remove color casts or enhance the color vibrancy.

Adjusting contrast: Contrast refers to the difference between the light and dark areas of the image. Adjusting the contrast can help make the image look more dynamic.

Advanced Editing Techniques

Advanced editing techniques involve more complex manipulation of the image, such as retouching, compositing, and adding special effects. Here are some advanced editing techniques:

Retouching: Retouching involves removing blemishes, wrinkles, or other imperfections from the image. This can be done using tools such as the healing brush or clone stamp tool.

Compositing: Compositing involves combining multiple images into one to create a new image. This can be done using layer masks and blending modes.

Special effects: Special effects involve adding creative elements to the image, such as adding a vignette or creating a high-key or low-key effect.

Tips for Achieving a Consistent Editing Style

Achieving a consistent editing style is essential for creating a cohesive body of work. Here are some tips for achieving a consistent editing style:

Develop a style: Developing a style involves deciding on the overall look and feel you want to achieve in your images. This could be a specific color palette or a particular editing technique.

Use presets: Presets are pre-defined editing settings that can be applied to multiple images. Using presets can help you achieve a consistent editing style across multiple images.

Create a workflow: Creating a workflow involves establishing a sequence of steps for editing your images. This can help you streamline your editing process and achieve a consistent style.

Practice, practice, practice: Consistency in editing takes time and practice. Experiment with different techniques and styles to find what works best for you and your images.

In conclusion, post-processing is a crucial part of digital photography, and understanding different post-processing techniques and software can help you create visually stunning images. Basic editing techniques involve adjusting the exposure, color, and contrast of the image, while advanced editing techniques involve more complex manipulation of the image.

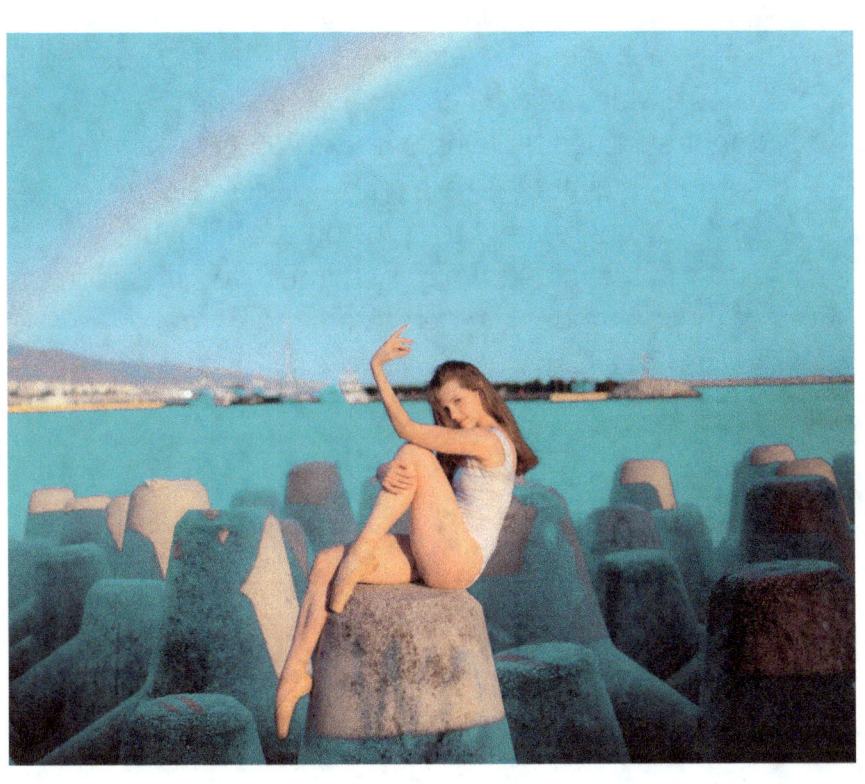

Chapter 9: Specialized Photography

Photography is a fascinating art form that allows individuals to capture moments, scenes, and subjects in a visual format. It is a versatile medium that can be used to convey a wide range of emotions, tell stories, and document experiences. One of the great things about photography is that there are many specialized genres that allow photographers to focus on specific types of subjects and techniques. In this chapter, we will explore four of the most popular specialized photography genres: portrait, landscape, wildlife, and macro photography.

Portrait Photography:

Portrait photography is the art of capturing a person's likeness, personality, and character in a still image. It is one of the most common types of photography and is often used for family portraits, senior pictures, and headshots for actors and models. A good portrait photograph should capture the essence of the subject's personality and convey a sense of their character.

One of the key elements of portrait photography is lighting. A skilled portrait photographer will use a combination of natural light and artificial light to create a flattering and dramatic effect on the subject. The photographer must also be able to direct the subject to achieve the desired expression, posture, and positioning.

Another important aspect of portrait photography is the choice of background. The background should be simple and unobtrusive, allowing the subject to be the focus of the image. The photographer may choose to use a plain white or black background, or a textured backdrop that complements the subject's clothing or personality.

Landscape Photography:

Landscape photography is the art of capturing the beauty and grandeur of natural landscapes, such as mountains, forests, and seascapes. It is a popular genre among nature enthusiasts and travel photographers who seek to document the majesty of the natural world.

One of the key elements of landscape photography is composition. A skilled landscape photographer will use a combination of elements, such as foreground, middle ground, and background, to create a balanced and visually appealing image. The photographer must also be able to select the right time of day and weather conditions to capture the desired mood and atmosphere.

Another important aspect of landscape photography is the use of filters. Filters can be used to enhance the colors and contrast in the image, or to create special effects such as long exposure shots of waterfalls or star trails.

Wildlife Photography:

Wildlife photography is the art of capturing images of animals in their natural habitat. It requires patience, skill, and a deep understanding of animal behavior. Wildlife photographers often travel to remote locations to capture images of rare and exotic animals.

One of the key elements of wildlife photography is understanding animal behavior. The photographer must be able to anticipate the animal's movements and behavior in order to capture the perfect shot. They must also be able to approach the animal without disturbing it or endangering themselves.

Another important aspect of wildlife photography is the use of telephoto lenses. Telephoto lenses allow the photographer to get close-up shots of the animal without disturbing its natural behavior. They also allow the photographer to blur the background, creating a shallow depth of field that emphasizes the subject.

Macro Photography:

Macro photography is the art of capturing extreme close-up images of small objects, such as flowers, insects, and other tiny subjects. It requires specialized equipment, such as macro lenses and extension tubes, to capture the detail and texture of the subject.

One of the key elements of macro photography is depth of field. Because the subject is so close to the camera, even a small aperture setting may not be enough to create a sharp image. The photographer may need to use focus stacking techniques to combine multiple images with different focus points to create a sharp image from front to back.

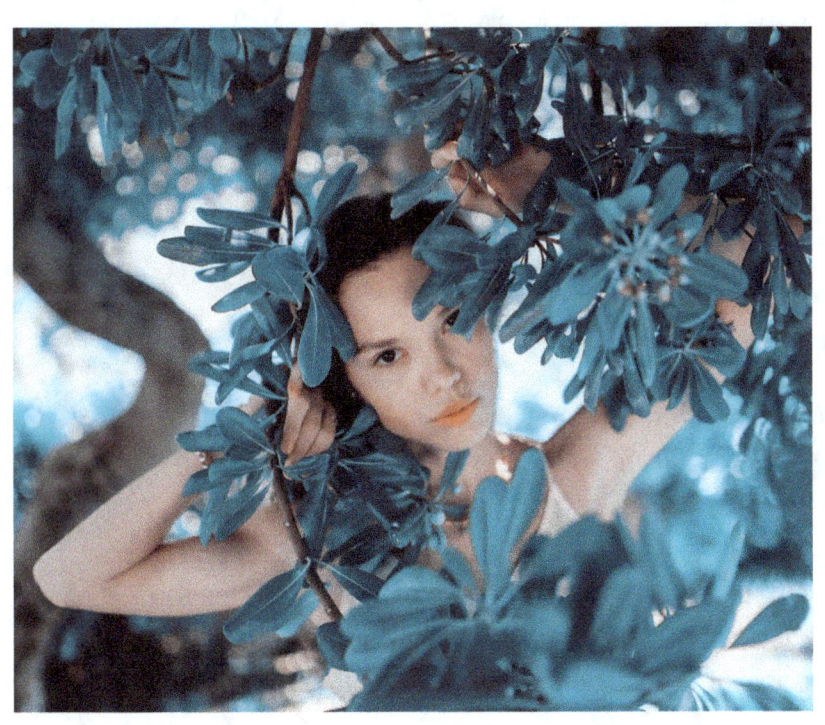

Chapter 10: Tips for Becoming a Better Photographer

Photography is an art form that requires skill, practice, and creativity. Whether you are a beginner or an experienced photographer, there is always room for improvement. In this chapter, we will explore some tips and techniques for becoming a better photographer, including the importance of practice, learning from others, experimenting with different techniques, and overcoming creative blocks.

Practice, Practice, Practice:

The most important tip for becoming a better photographer is to practice. Photography is a skill that requires practice to master. The more you practice, the better you will become. Take your camera with you wherever you go and look for opportunities to take pictures. Try different settings, angles, and lighting conditions to see what works best for you.

Another way to practice is to set up a photo challenge for yourself. Choose a specific theme or subject and try to capture it in different ways. For example, you could challenge yourself to take 10 different photos of the same flower, each one with a different angle or lighting condition. This will help you to develop your skills and find your own style.

Learn From Others:

One of the best ways to improve your photography skills is to learn from others. Take classes, attend workshops, and read books and blogs on photography. You can also learn from other photographers by studying their work and asking for feedback.

Networking with other photographers is also a great way to learn. Join a photography club or group, attend meetups, or participate in online forums. This will give you the opportunity to share your work, get feedback, and learn from others.

Experiment with Different Techniques:

Photography is a versatile medium that allows you to experiment with different techniques and styles. Try shooting in black and white, using different types of lenses, or playing with different types of lighting. You can also experiment with post-processing techniques, such as cropping, color correction, and filters.

Another way to experiment is to try different types of photography. If you typically shoot landscapes, try shooting portraits or wildlife. This will help you to develop your skills in different areas and find new ways to express your creativity.

Tips for Overcoming Creative Blocks:

Even the most experienced photographers can experience creative blocks from time to time. Here are some tips for overcoming creative blocks and finding inspiration:

Take a break: Sometimes, the best thing you can do is take a break from photography. Take some time to recharge and do something else that you enjoy. This will help you to come back to photography with a fresh perspective.

Look for inspiration: Look for inspiration in other forms of art, such as painting, music, or literature. You can also look for inspiration in nature, architecture, or everyday objects.

Try something new: Sometimes, trying something new can help you to overcome a creative block. Try shooting with a different lens, experimenting with a new technique, or shooting in a different location.

Collaborate with others: Collaborating with other photographers or artists can help you to find new ideas and inspiration. You can work together on a project or share ideas and feedback.

Set goals: Setting goals can help you to stay motivated and focused. Set a goal for yourself, such as shooting a certain number of photos per day or week, or completing a specific project within a certain timeframe.

In conclusion, becoming a better photographer takes time, practice, and dedication. By practicing regularly, learning from others, experimenting with different techniques, and overcoming creative blocks, you can improve your skills and develop your own unique style. Remember to enjoy the process and have fun with photography!

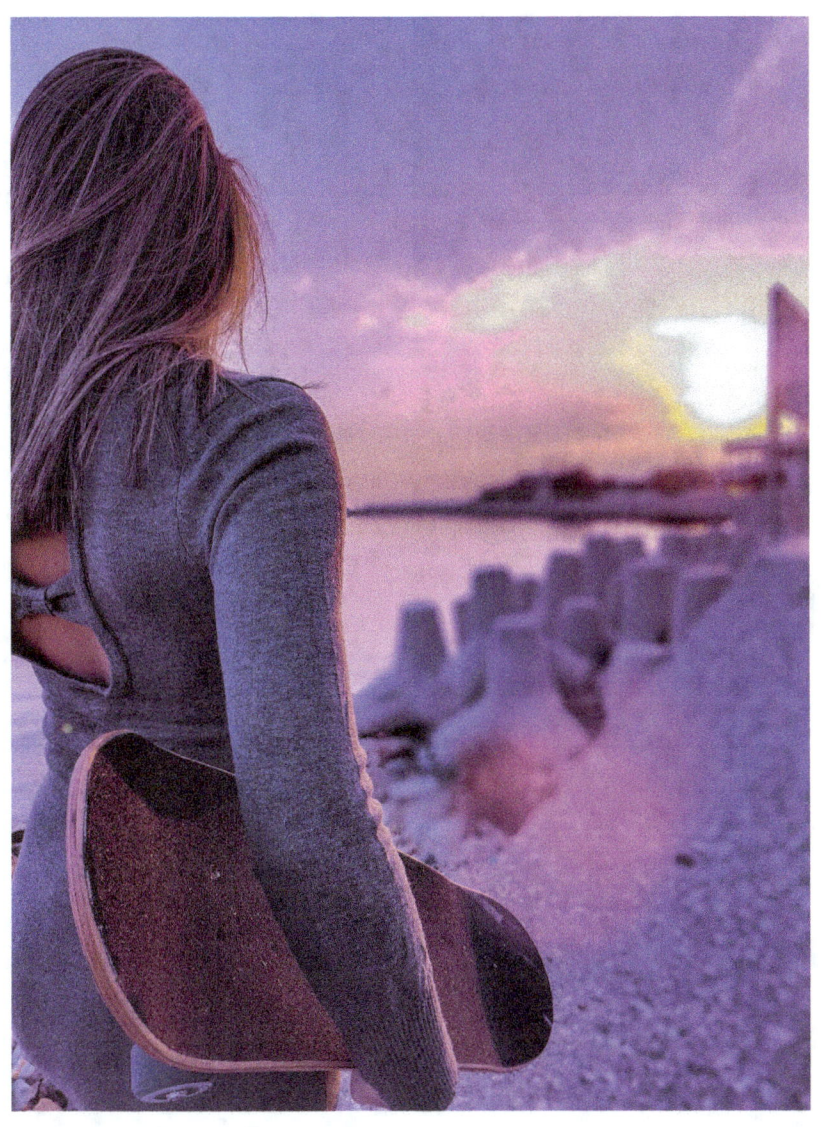

Bonus Chapter: How to Sell Your Photography & The Future of Photography

If you're a photographer, you may be interested in selling your work. There are many ways to sell your photography, including through online marketplaces, galleries, and print-on-demand services. In this chapter, we will explore some tips and strategies for selling your photography, including the growing trend of selling digital art through non-fungible tokens (NFTs).

Build a Portfolio

Before you can start selling your photography, you need to build a portfolio that showcases your best work. Choose your best images and organize them in a way that highlights your skills and style. Make sure your portfolio is accessible online, either through your own website or through a platform like Behance or Flickr.

Understand the Market

To sell your photography successfully, you need to understand the market and what buyers are looking for. Research different types of photography and the demand for each. Look at what other photographers are selling and what prices they are charging. This will help you to set realistic prices and create images that appeal to buyers.

Choose a Sales Platform

There are many platforms you can use to sell your photography, including online marketplaces like Etsy and Shutterstock, galleries, and print-on-demand services like Fine Art America and Redbubble. Consider the pros and cons of each platform and choose the one that is best suited for your needs.

Promote Your Work

To sell your photography, you need to promote it. Share your work on social media, your website, and any other relevant platforms. Use hashtags to make your images more discoverable and consider reaching out to influencers or other photographers for collaborations or partnerships.

Offer Limited Edition Prints

One way to increase the value of your photography is to offer limited edition prints. This creates a sense of exclusivity and can help to drive up prices. Consider limiting the number of prints you make or offering signed and numbered prints.

Consider NFTs

Non-fungible tokens (NFTs) are a growing trend in the world of digital art. Essentially, an NFT is a digital certificate of ownership that verifies the authenticity and uniqueness of a digital artwork. This has opened up new opportunities for photographers to sell their work as digital art. Platforms like Nifty Gateway, SuperRare, and OpenSea allow photographers to sell their digital art as NFTs.

In conclusion, selling your photography takes time and effort, but it can be a rewarding way to earn income from your passion. By building a strong portfolio, understanding the market, choosing the right sales platform, promoting your work, offering limited edition prints, and considering the use of NFTs, you can increase your chances of success in the photography industry.

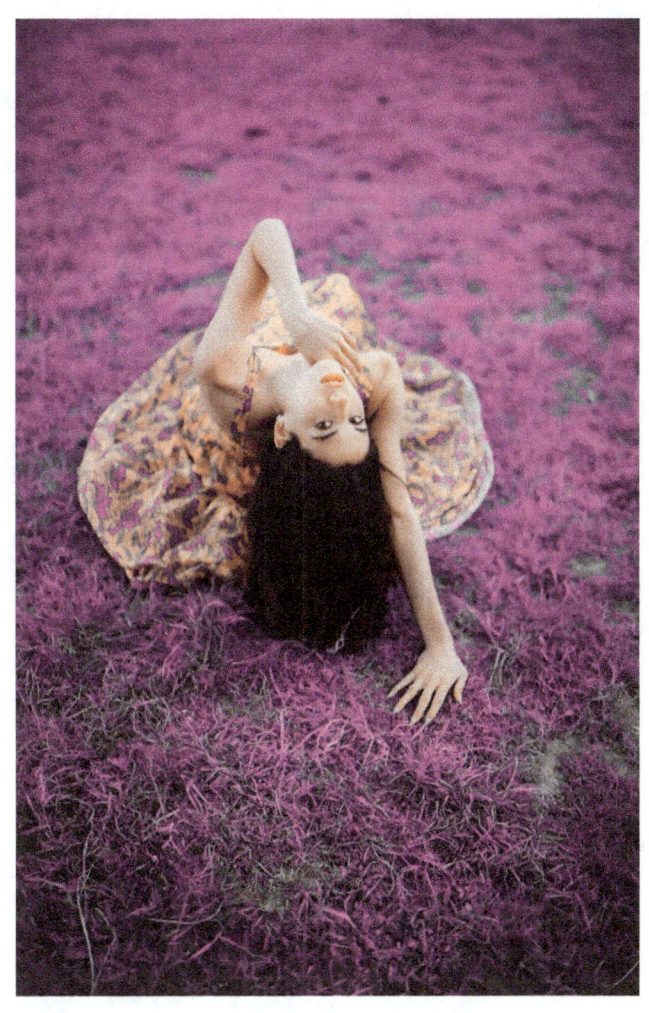

The Future of Photography

Photography has come a long way since its invention in the early 19th century. Today, it is a ubiquitous part of our lives, with billions of photos being taken every day. With the advancement of technology, photography has become more accessible than ever before, and the future of photography is exciting. In this chapter, we will explore some of the trends that are shaping the future of photography.

Artificial Intelligence and Machine Learning
Artificial intelligence (AI) and machine learning (ML) are transforming the way we take and edit photos. AI algorithms can be used to enhance the quality of an image, remove unwanted elements, and even create entirely new images. With the help of machine learning, cameras can learn from their mistakes and improve their performance, making it easier for photographers to capture the perfect shot.

Augmented Reality

Augmented reality (AR) is another technology that is transforming the world of photography. With AR, photographers can create immersive experiences that combine the real world with virtual elements. This technology has already been used in apps like Snapchat and Instagram, allowing users to add filters and animations to their photos and videos.

Virtual Reality

Virtual reality (VR) is another technology that is having a significant impact on photography. With VR, photographers can create immersive experiences that transport viewers to different places and environments. This technology has already been used to create virtual tours of museums, historic sites, and natural wonders.

360-Degree Cameras

360-degree cameras are becoming increasingly popular, allowing photographers to capture immersive images and videos that provide a complete view of a scene. This technology is particularly useful in fields like real estate, where potential buyers can take virtual tours of properties.

Drones

Drones have revolutionized the way we take photos and videos from the air, making it easier to capture stunning aerial shots. With the help of drones, photographers can capture images from angles that were previously impossible, opening up new creative possibilities.

Computational Photography

Computational photography is a new field that uses software algorithms to enhance the quality of images. This technology can be used to remove noise, blur, and other imperfections, making it easier to capture sharp and clear images.

Wearable Cameras

Wearable cameras are becoming increasingly popular, allowing photographers to capture images and videos from a first-person perspective. This technology has already been used in fields like extreme sports, allowing athletes to capture their experiences in a unique and immersive way.

Social Media

Social media has had a significant impact on the way we take and share photos. Platforms like Instagram and Snapchat have made it easier than ever to share images with a global audience, creating new opportunities for photographers to showcase their work and build their brand.

Sustainability

As concerns about the environment grow, sustainability is becoming an increasingly important issue in the photography industry. Manufacturers are now producing cameras and accessories that are more environmentally friendly, while photographers are exploring new ways to create images that have a smaller carbon footprint.

Personalization

Personalization is another trend that is shaping the future of photography. With the help of AI and machine learning, cameras can learn a photographer's preferences and adjust their settings accordingly, making it easier to capture the perfect shot.

As the concept of the metaverse gains momentum, it is likely to have a significant impact on the world of photography. The metaverse is a term used to describe a collective virtual shared space, created by the convergence of physical and virtual reality. In the metaverse, users will be able to interact with each other and with virtual objects in a seamless and immersive way.

One way that photography is likely to be impacted by the metaverse is through virtual photography. Just as photographers capture images of the physical world, virtual photographers will be able to capture images of the virtual world within the metaverse. These images will be used to document virtual events, locations, and experiences, and will play a critical role in shaping the metaverse's culture and identity.

Virtual photography will require a new set of skills and tools. Photographers will need to become familiar with the virtual environment and the tools and techniques required to capture high-quality images within it. They will need to understand lighting, composition, and framing within the virtual world, and will need to develop new techniques for post-processing and editing virtual images.

Another way that the metaverse is likely to impact photography is through the creation of new virtual experiences. Just as photographers create images that evoke emotion and tell a story, virtual experiences within the metaverse will aim to create immersive and memorable experiences for users. These experiences may be created through a combination of virtual photography, animation, and other media, and will be designed to transport users to new and exciting virtual worlds.

In addition to virtual photography, the metaverse is likely to have an impact on traditional photography as well. As virtual experiences become more prevalent, photographers may find new opportunities to capture images of people and places within the metaverse that are relevant to the physical world. For example, a virtual concert may be documented through traditional photography to provide a record of the event for those who were not able to attend in person.

In conclusion, the metaverse is likely to have a significant impact on the world of photography. Virtual photography will become an essential skill, requiring photographers to adapt to the virtual environment and develop new techniques and tools. Virtual experiences within the metaverse will create new opportunities for photographers to capture images that evoke emotion and tell a story. The metaverse is an exciting and rapidly evolving area, and it will be interesting to see how photography evolves alongside it.

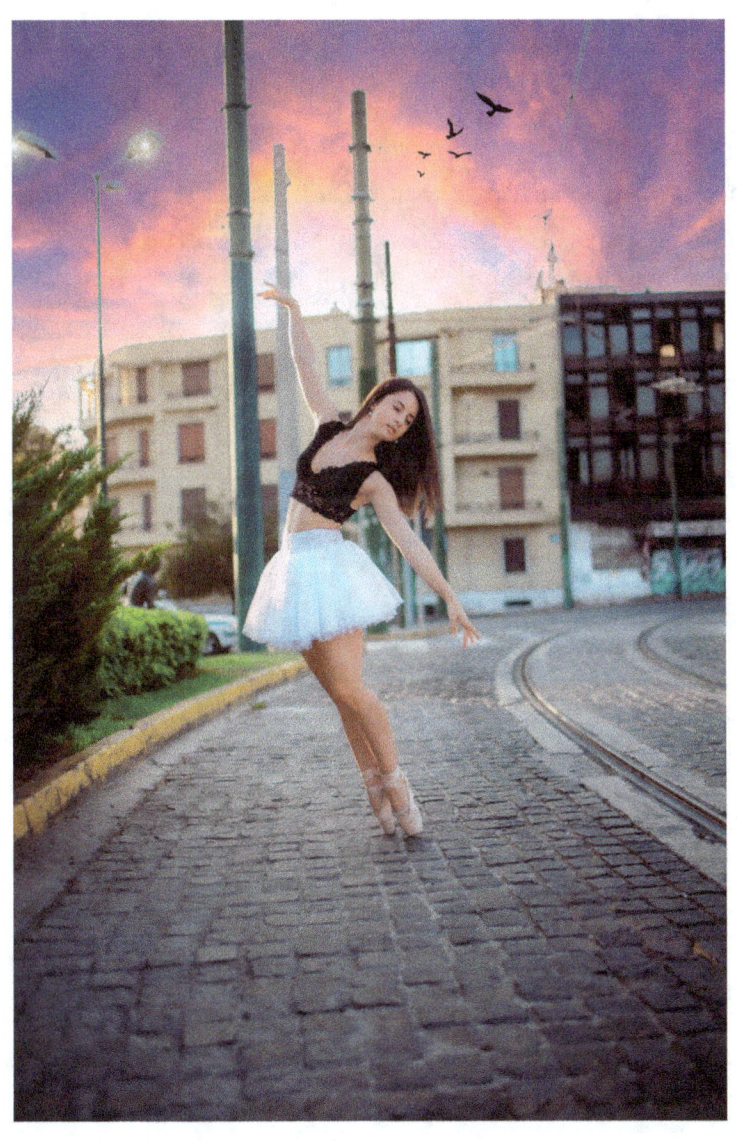

Conclusion

Photography is a powerful art form that allows us to capture and preserve memories, tell stories, and document important events. Over the years, photography has evolved significantly, with the invention of new technologies and advancements in camera technology. Today, we have a wide range of cameras available, from high-end DSLRs to smartphones with impressive cameras.

In this e-book, we have explored the different types of photography, understanding your camera and its features, composition and framing techniques, and lighting tips and tricks. We have learned how to take stunning photos that capture our vision and tell our story.

As we look to the future, we can expect to see significant advancements in photography, including the emergence of artificial intelligence (AI) and machine learning. These technologies will enable cameras to analyze and interpret images in real-time, and automatically adjust settings to optimize image quality.

Photography is an essential tool for businesses, allowing them to market and promote their products and services effectively. It also has a significant impact on our emotions and how we perceive the world around us. Photography can evoke strong emotions, evoke memories, and tell powerful stories.

In conclusion, photography is an art form that will continue to evolve and change over time. It is a tool that allows us to capture and preserve our memories, document important events, and tell stories. With the advancements in technology, we can look forward to capturing even more incredible moments and creating beautiful images that inspire and move us.

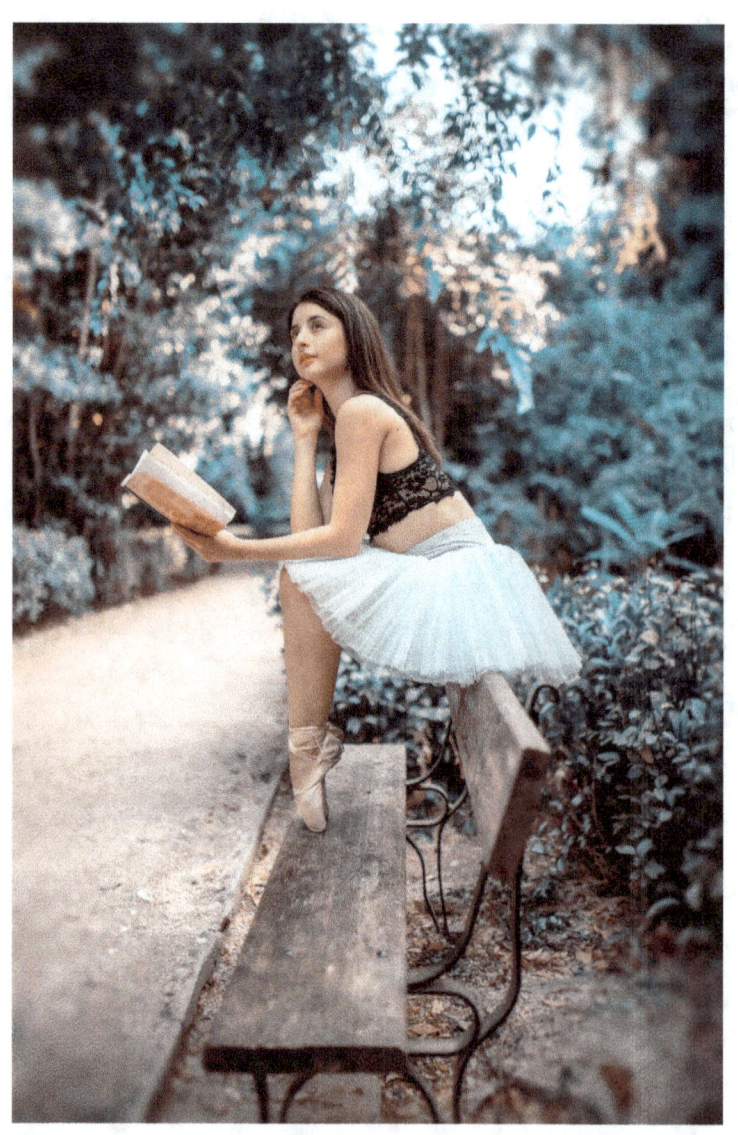

Dear Readers,

As I come to the end of this book, I want to take a moment to express my sincere gratitude to each and every one of you. Thank you for taking the time to read this book and for allowing me to share my knowledge and passion for photography with you.

I hope that the information and tips in this book have been helpful to you in your photography journey. Whether you are a beginner just starting out or a seasoned professional, my goal has been to provide you with valuable insights and inspiration to help you improve your skills and take your photography to the next level.

It has been an honor and a pleasure to share my expertise with you, and I am grateful for the opportunity to connect with you through this book. I hope that you have found it informative, engaging, and enjoyable to read.

Again, thank you for your support and for choosing to read my book. I wish you all the best in your photography endeavors and hope that you continue to pursue your passion with enthusiasm and creativity.

I also want to take this opportunity to let you know that all of the photographs featured in this book were taken by me. As a photographer, I believe that images speak louder than words, and I wanted to showcase my own work as a way to inspire and educate you.

Special Thanks
Book Cover Photo: Model Fotini Antoniadi

www.ivphotographylab.com

Nickos IV